This Book Belongs to

_____

- - - - - - - - - - - - - - - - - - -

_____

advantage
speech therapy services

OF SPEECH

Companion Book

Robyn M. Drothler, M.ED CCC-SLP

Table of Contents

Dedication

I dedicate this book to all the kids and families
I have served over the last 27 years!

There have been so many lessons that have helped
shape this book into what it is!

How to Use This Book

1. The order of the pages is strategic in that easier skills are in the beginning and should progressively get harder as you move through it.

2. I encourage you to take the ideas off each page and think of more items 'Like the ones" provided. The examples on the pages are simply just examples for YOU to use and expand on the skill

3. Blank pages are provided in the back to take notes, document progress, or add any ideas you may want to elaborate on.

4. While older kids will be able to read the directions and be more independent, younger kids can do the same work as long as someone works with them. Read the directions, talk about it, and then have them 'do' the task verbally. Therefore, any "receptive" task (i.e. text or written) can be turned into an "expressive" task (verbally spoken) simply by talking about it.

5. Kids work at their own pace and some skills (despite the order) may be easier or harder for any individual child - and that's ok.

6. Each page has a skill listed at the bottom for the main skill being addressed on that page. You can go to the INDEX in the back to see how the skills overlap on the different pages and use it as a quick guide to find the activities you want to work on.

Practice makes progress!!

Definitions:

RECEPTIVE LANGUAGE - the language your child understands when you talk to them or give them a direction.

EXPRESSIVE LANGUAGE - the language your child uses verbally. It represents the words your child is capable of using to label and identify objects as well as express wants and needs.

ARTICULATION is the ability to produce different sounds. Your child's speech intelligibility is based on their ability to articulate their words.

VOICE DISORDER is any variation in pitch, intensity, quality etc that draws unfavorable attention (i.e. hoarseness).

FLUENCY is any interruption in the flow of oral language (repetitions, prolongations etc). *For younger children, there is a level of 'normal disfluency' when they are learning to speak - yet - if they get stuck or block on the words as they are trying to speak you may want to have your child tested.

About the Author
Robyn Drothler, M.ED CCC-SLP

Robyn Drothler is the owner of Advantage Speech Therapy Services Inc. (ASTS).

She graduated from the College of Wooster (Ohio) in 1995 with an undergraduate degree in Communication Sciences and Disorders and a minor in Psychology.

She worked for three years in the Manatee County School District in Florida. In May 2000, Robyn graduated from Valdosta State University with a Master's in Education.

During three years in Gwinnett County, GA, post-graduate, she earned her Certificate of Clinical Competence while also working for private therapy companies. In 2002, Robyn founded ASTS.

Robyn is a certified member of ASHA, The American Speech-Language-Hearing Association, and state certified in Georgia. She continues expanding and developing her knowledge and skills post-graduate with continuing education courses.

Robyn is experienced in, but not limited to, Articulation / Phono-logical disorders, Developmental Delays, Autism / PDD, and Down Syndrome.

Speech Sound Development

Speech Sound Norms taken from the
Goldman Fristoe Test of Articulation-2 from 2000.

Age	Initial Sound	Medial Sound	Final Sound
2 years	/b/ /d/ /h/ /m/ /n/ /p/	/b/ /m/ /n/	/m/ /p/
3 years	/f/ /g/ /k/ /t/ /w/	/f/ /g/ /k/ ng /p/ /t/	/b/ /d/ /g/ /k/ /n/ /t/
4 years	/kw/	/d/	/f/
5 years	ch j /l/ /s/ sh y /bl/	ch j /l/ /s/ sh /z/	/l/ ng ch j /s/ sh /ɾ/ /v/ /z/
6 years	/ɾ/ /v/ /bɾ/ /dɾ/ /fl/ /fɾ/ /gl/ /gɾ/ /kl/ /kɾ/ /pl/ /st/ /tɾ/	/ɾ/ /v/	
7 years	/z/ /sl/ /sp/ /sw/ th	th	th

This table is the age at which 85% of the GFTA-2 Standardization Sample
correctly produced the consonant and consonant cluster sounds.

Resources

☑ To find a professional in your area - Go to https://www.asha.org/profind/

☑ Check with your insurance company for in-network providers. When asking about coverage, don't just ask if you have coverage or not for speech therapy; make sure you ask whether or not you have a) in network coverage b) if the diagnosis is covered, and c) where the coverage allows (home, school/daycare, teletherapy)

☑ To view additional resources from Advantage Speech - go to https://advantagespeech.com/resources-child-development- and-speech-therapy/

☑ To go more in depth and learn more about speech therapy and behaviors associated with how kids communicate, go to www.go.advantagespeech.com.

☑ For developmental milestones for your child's age/grade level, go to https://www.asha.org/public/speech/development/ kindergarten/

☑ For additional resources about speech development from ASHA go to https://www.asha.org/public/speech/development/

Action

Bb

Behavior

Carryover

Details

Everyday Teachable Moments

Friends and Family

Greetings

High Fives

Include

Joking

Kk

Key = Consistency

CHILDREN'S SECTION

Good Night Moon

Brown Bear Brown Bear

Ll

Library

M m

MONKEY

Mirror

Narrator/Narrate

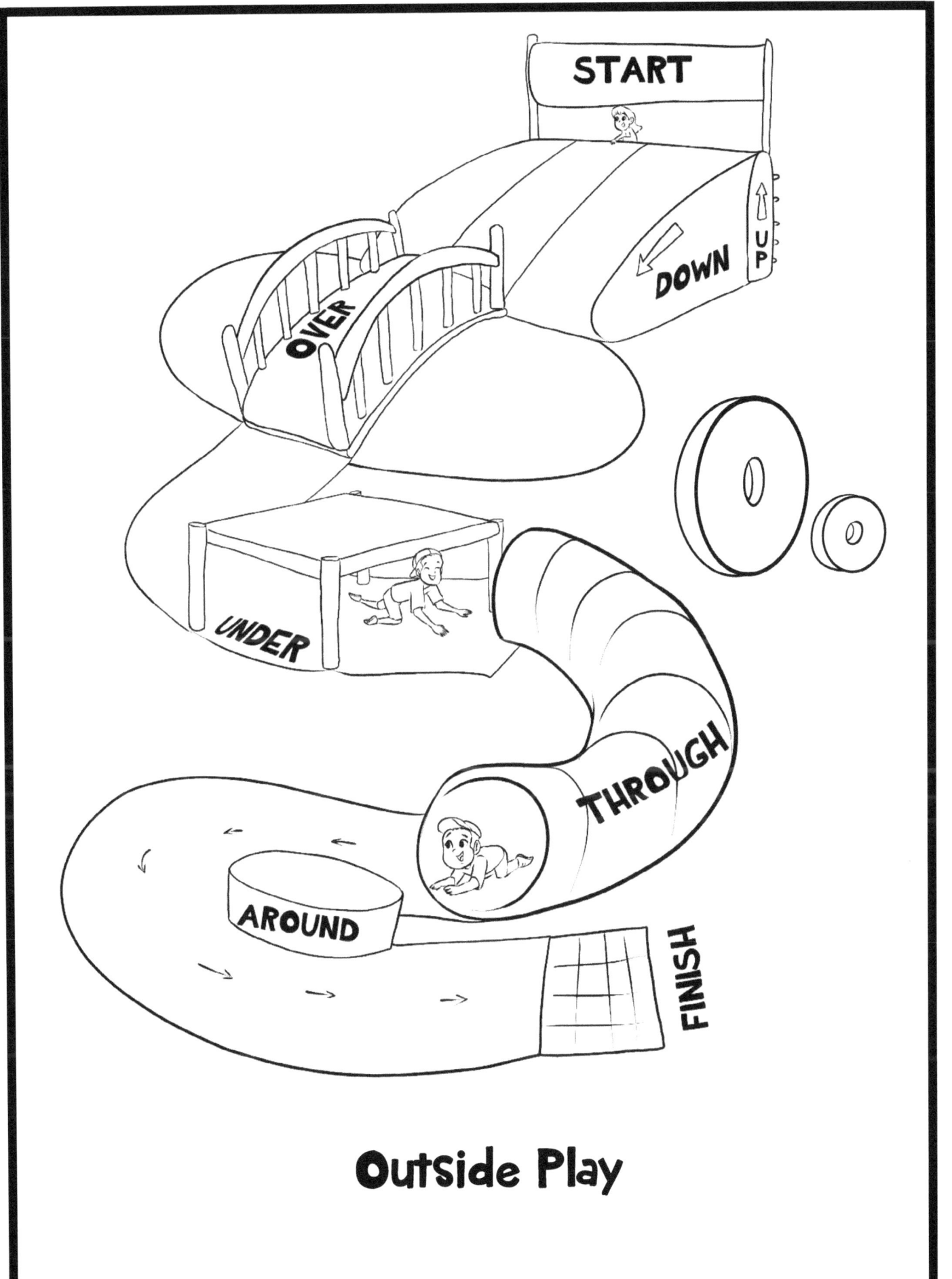

Outside Play

PECS
Picture Exchange Communication System

Questions

Sign Language

Understand

Daily Schedule Chart

Breakfast	
Get Dressed	
Brush Teeth	
School	
Homework	 
Speech	
Dinner	
Family Time	
Bed Time	

Visuals

Be ♡ Kind to everyone

Ww

Welcome
New Ideas

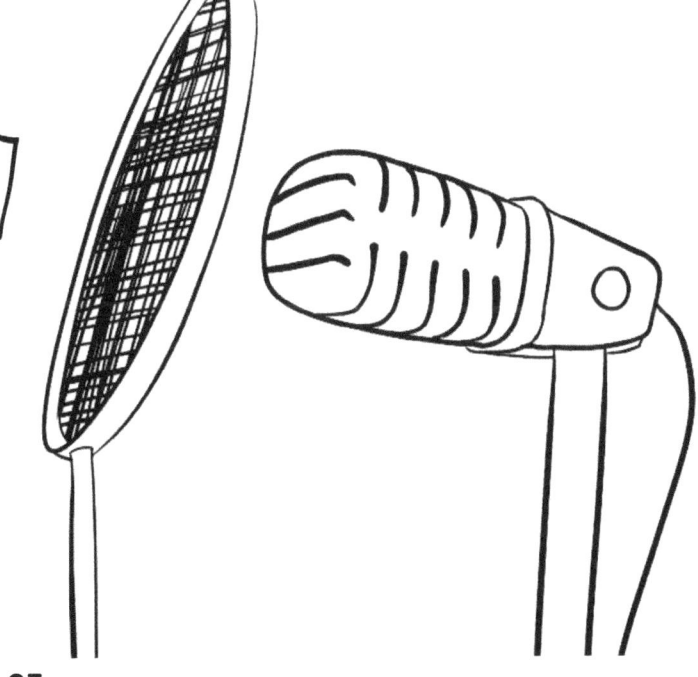

You Have Two Choices

Exaggerate
(This word makes the "Z" sound)

Letter Recognition Game for Capitals and Lowercase

Pick a handful of capitals and corresponding lowercase letters. Put capitals in one row and lowercase in another on the floor.

One person puts their foot on the capital letter and the person on the other side, puts their foot on the corresponding lowercase version of that target letter.

You can increase the complexity by putting a timer on it. Be sure to switch places so each person can be both the and the follower.

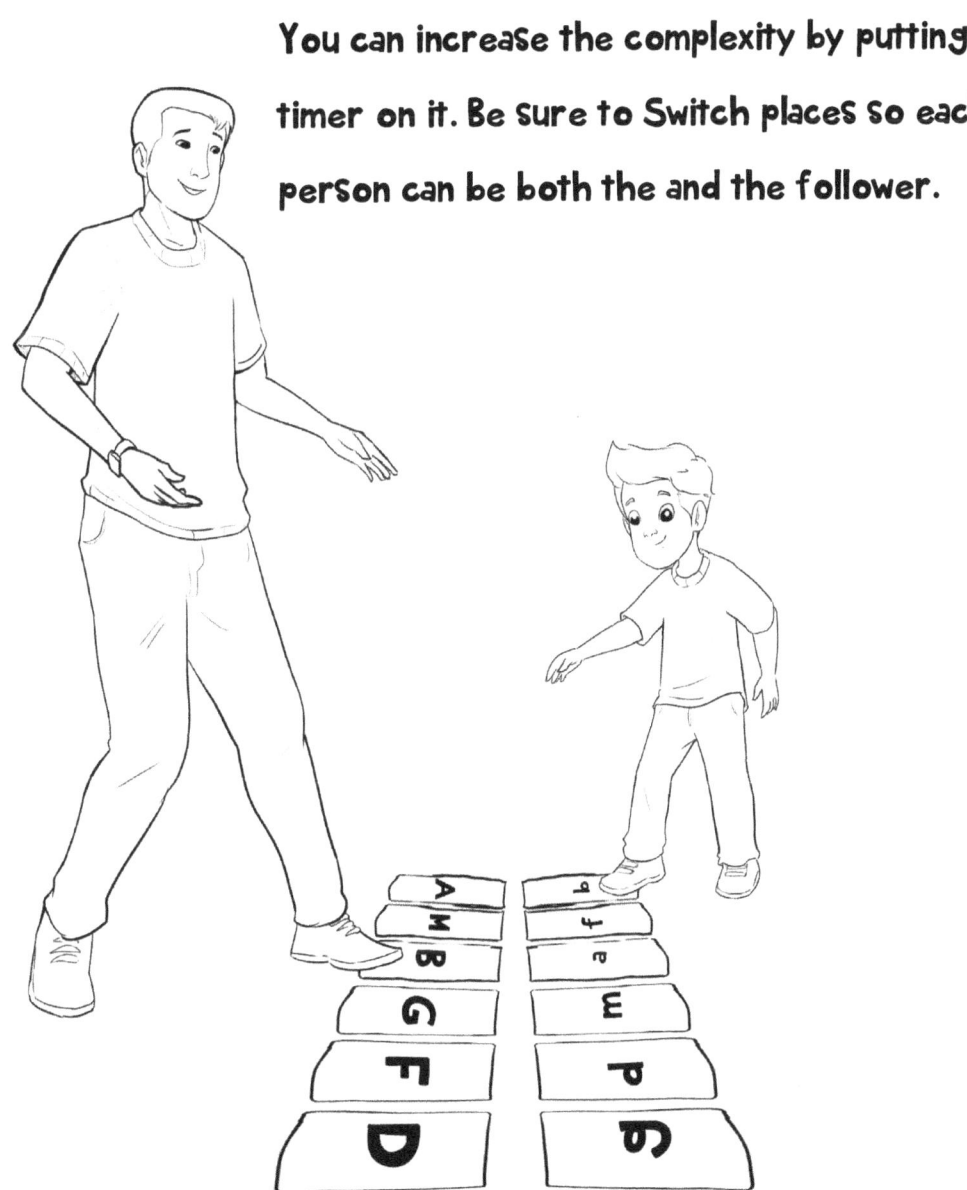

Skill: Expressing Wants and Needs

When using ABC puzzles, think about the following:

*Connecting the removable letter to the space where the letter goes.

*Connecting the removable letter to the picture that starts with that letter.

*Reinforce the letter sound by practicing the sound when you hold up the letter.

*Have the child find the letter that makes the targeted sound.

*Describe the object you want them to find if they cannot find something that starts with that letter. Ex. I see something we eat, its red, its a fruit, grows on trees, and has seeds in the middle. APPLE!

*You could say I'm looking for something **NEXT TO** the "moon" or **BELOW** the "carrot". Find me the "zipper" at the **END** of the puzzle.

Trace the letters and at the end write your name

A a B b

A a   A a   A a   A a   A a

A a   A a   A a   A a   A a

A a   A a   A a   A a   A a

B b   B b   B b   B b   B b

B b   B b   B b   B b   B b

B b   B b   B b   B b   B b

Cc   Dd   Ee

Cc Cc Cc Cc Cc

Cc Cc Cc Cc Cc

Cc Cc Cc Cc Cc

Dd Dd Dd Dd Dd

Dd Dd Dd Dd Dd

Dd Dd Dd Dd Dd

Ee Ee Ee Ee Ee

Ee Ee Ee Ee Ee

Ee Ee Ee Ee Ee

Ff   Gg   Hh

Ff Ff Ff Ff Ff Ff

Ff Ff Ff Ff Ff Ff

Ff Ff Ff Ff Ff Ff

Gg Gg Gg Gg Gg

Gg Gg Gg Gg Gg

Gg Gg Gg Gg Gg

Hh Hh Hh Hh Hh

Hh Hh Hh Hh Hh

Hh Hh Hh Hh Hh

Ii   Jj   Kk

Ll   Mm   Nn

Oo   Pp   Qq

Oo Oo Oo Oo Oo

Oo Oo Oo Oo Oo

Oo Oo Oo Oo Oo

Pp Pp Pp Pp Pp

Pp Pp Pp Pp Pp

Pp Pp Pp Pp Pp

Qq Qq Qq Qq Qq

Qq Qq Qq Qq Qq

Qq Qq Qq Qq Qq

Rr   Ss   Tt

Uu   Vv   Ww

Xx   Yy   Zz

37

Now, write your name.

Good Job!

ASL - American Sign Language
Match the word to the sign

Thirsty

More

Eat

Thank you

Hungry

ASL - American Sign Language
Match the word to the sign

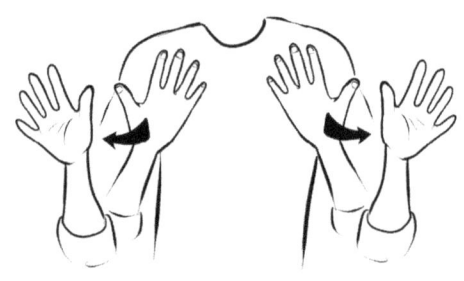

Please

Drink

All done

Sleepy

Good night

Skill: Expressing Wants and Needs

ASL - American Sign Language

Match the word to the sign

Sorry

Water

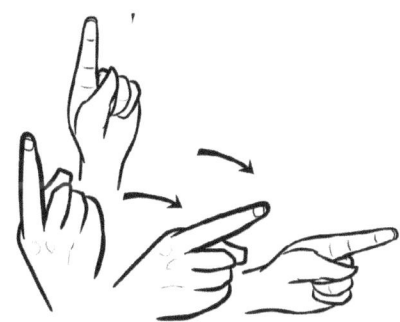

Go

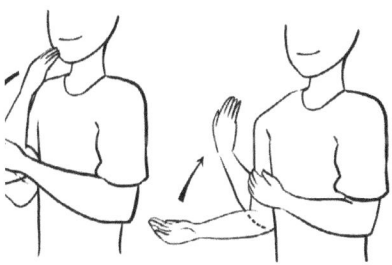

Good morning

Drive a Car

Bathroom

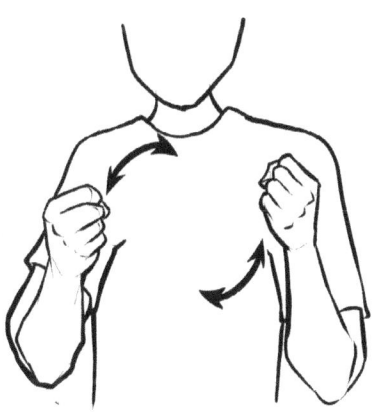

Find the Circles

Find the Squares

Find the Triangles

Find the Rectangles

Skill: Shape Recognition

45

Match the Letter sound with the pictures.

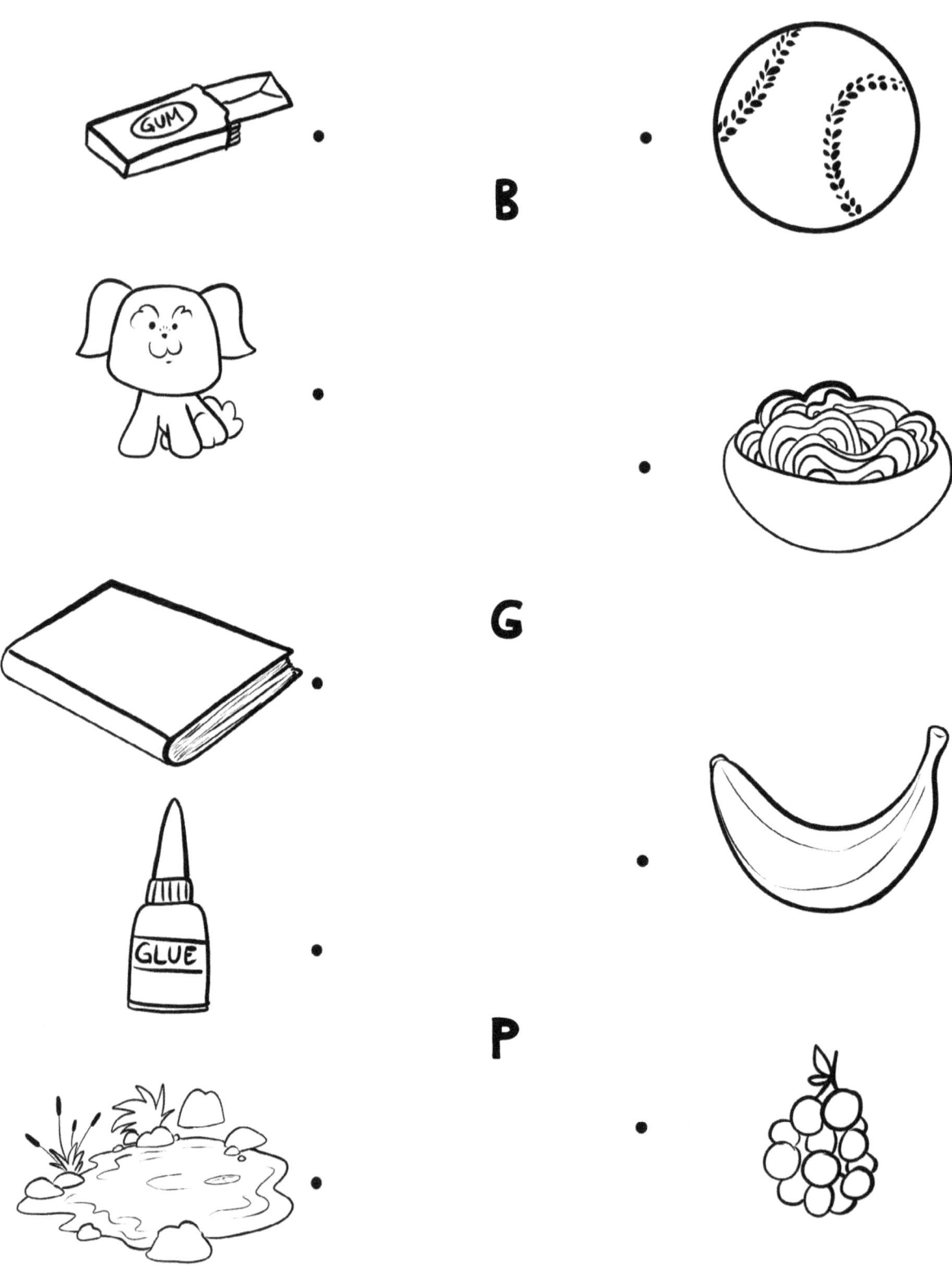

B

G

P

Match the Letter sound with the pictures.

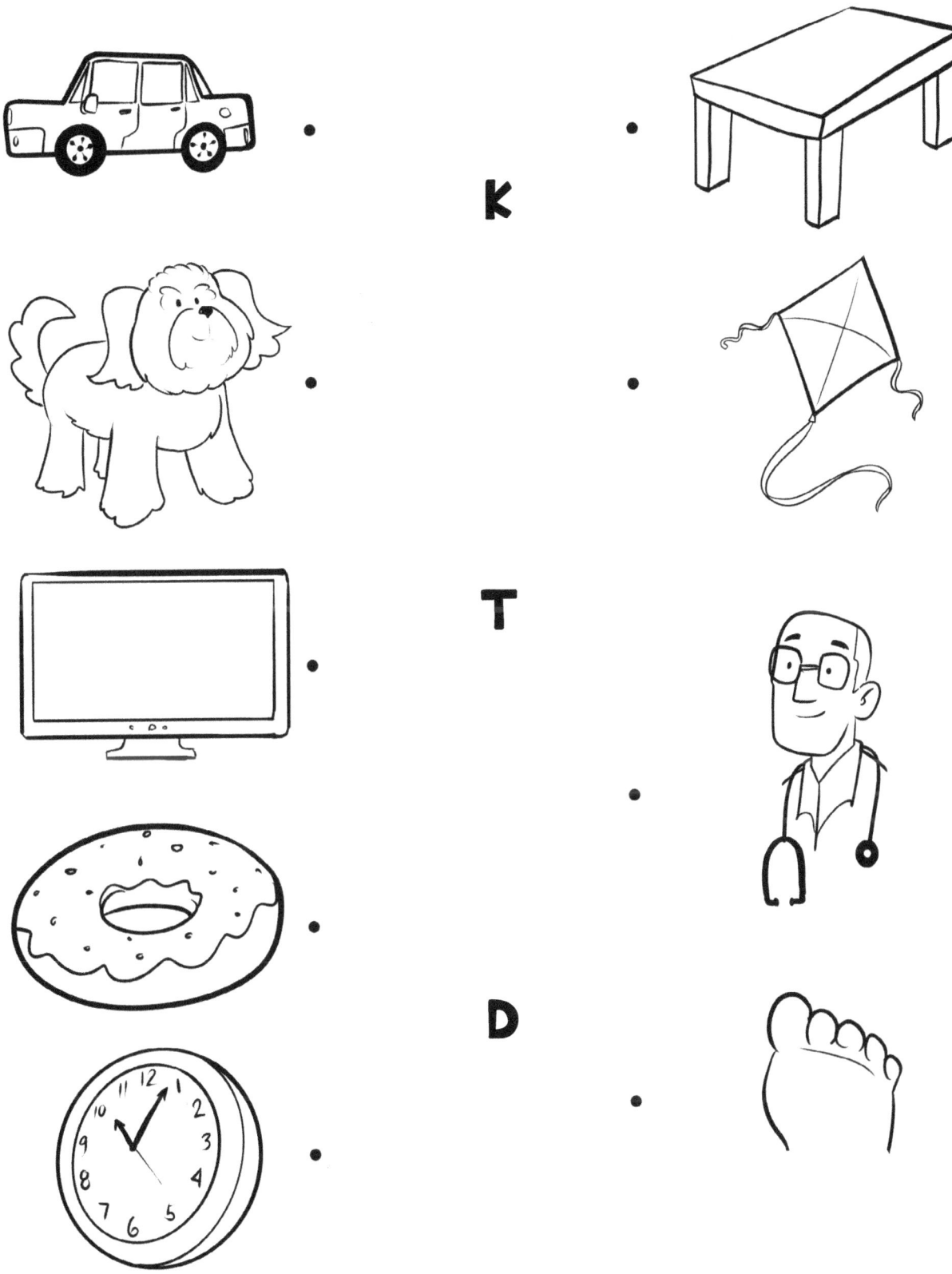

K

T

D

Match the Letter sound with the pictures.

S

V

F

End Here →

← Start Here

Skill: Sequencing.

49

Day in the Life Maze
Write out the steps of how you made it through the maze.

_____
_____
_____
_____
_____
_____
_____
_____
_____
_____
_____
_____
_____
_____
_____
_____
_____
_____
_____
_____
_____
_____
_____
_____
_____

Day in the Life Maze

Draw 6 different things you do in a day.

1	2
3	4
5	6

Princess	Parking Lot	Carwash	Kid
Panda	Pasta	Cat	T-Shirt
Pig	Picnic	Car	Tornado
Porcupine	Party Hat	Carrot	Toad
Potato		Cookie	Tree

Skill: Receptive Vocabulary & Symantic Absurdities.

Turtle	Basket	Monkey	Dinosaur
Tea	Blanket	Money	Dragon
Table	Bottle	Milk	Donuts
Umbrella	Bowl	Mommy	Farm
Zoo	Baby Monkey	Gorilla	

Go Togethers
Draw a line to match the things that go together

What rhymes with _____?

Cat
1. _____
2. _____
3. _____

Ice
1. _____
2. _____
3. _____

Star
1. _____
2. _____
3. _____

Type
1. _____
2. _____
3. _____

Spoon
1. _____
2. _____
3. _____

Foam
1. _____
2. _____
3. _____

Bug
1. _____
2. _____
3. _____

Ran
1. _____
2. _____
3. _____

Lash
1. _____
2. _____
3. _____

Fair
1. _____
2. _____
3. _____

Skill: Rhyming

Opposites

Write the word under the picture and
match it to its opposite pair.

Hard

Soft

Fast

Slow

Awake

Asleep

Full

Empty

Fat

Skinny

Opposites

Write the word under the picture and
match it to its opposite pair.

Up

Down

Long

Short

Hot

Cold

Wet

Dry

Deep

Shallow

Skill: Grammar: Prepositions

57

Hopscotch

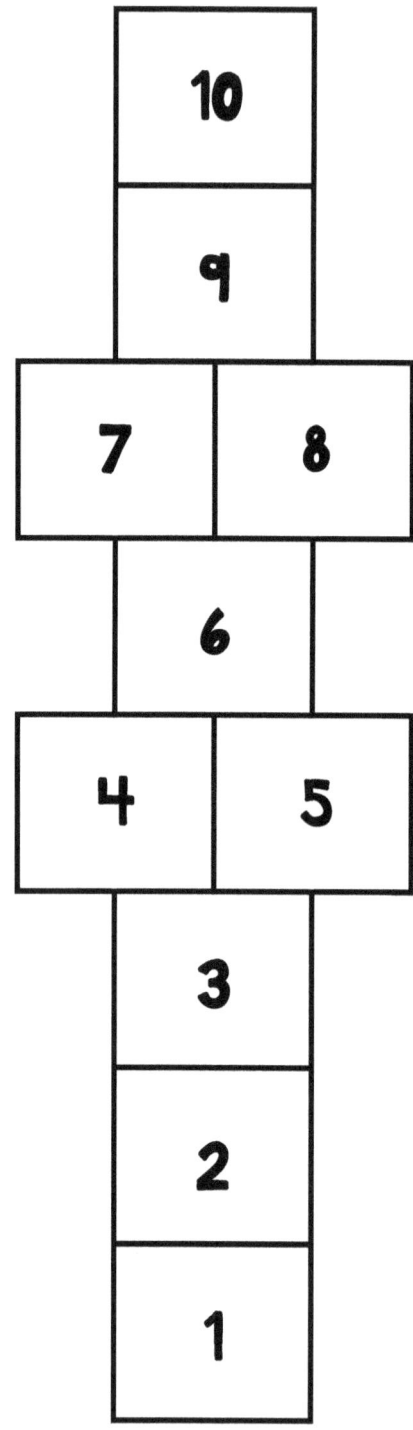

1.   Create the board with chalk on your driveway and number each box.

2.   Throw your rock on #1.
     If it touches the lines you lose your turn.

3.   Hop over the rock on the way to number 10, then turn around and hop back, picking up your rock along the way

4.   Continue with the remaining numbers by following the Same pattern. If you overthrow or lose your balance, then your turn ends.

The first one to complete the board wins.

Skill: Sequencing, Turn-taking, Number Identification, Following Directions, Physical Activity

Categories

Name Items in Each Category

Fruit

_____
_____
_____
_____
_____

Vegetables

_____
_____
_____
_____
_____

In the Sky

_____
_____
_____
_____
_____

Body Parts

_____
_____
_____
_____
_____

Tools

_____
_____
_____
_____
_____

Vehicles

_____
_____
_____
_____
_____

Toys

_____
_____
_____
_____
_____

Months

_____
_____
_____
_____
_____

Animals   (farm, zoo, ocean)

_____
_____
_____
_____
_____

Colors

_____
_____
_____
_____
_____

Furniture

_____
_____
_____
_____
_____

At the Beach

_____
_____
_____
_____
_____

Skill: Categorization

When Going to the Grocery Store

Ask Questions:

- Where do we find produce?
- What do we need with our cereal to make it complete? Where do we find the frozen foods?
- What can we eat for breakfast?

Make a list of items you need before you go to the store:

- Fruit
- Veggies
- Meat
- Snacks
- Frozen Foods
- Cleaning Supplies

Have your children give you directions around the store to find the items.

OR... You tell them where to go and See if they end up at the right place.

Example: Go straight, turn on aisle 3, it's on the top bottom shelf next to...

If you know your grocery store well enough, you could create a Scavenger hunt for them while they are there.

If your kids are different ages, you can have them work together in pairs.

Skill: Categorization, Following Directions

Lists

What do you need for:

Overnight bag/weekend away

_____   _____   _____

_____   _____   _____

_____   _____   _____

School Backpack

_____   _____   _____

_____   _____   _____

_____   _____   _____

Picnic

_____   _____   _____

_____   _____   _____

_____   _____   _____

Going to the Beach

_____   _____   _____

_____   _____   _____

_____   _____   _____

Lunch Bag

_____   _____   _____

_____   _____   _____

_____   _____   _____

Skill: Categorization

Scavenger Hunt

Find things in your house that start with the letter:

B _____ _____ _____ _____ _____

  _____ _____ _____ _____ _____

S _____ _____ _____ _____ _____

  _____ _____ _____ _____ _____

T _____ _____ _____ _____ _____

  _____ _____ _____ _____ _____

M _____ _____ _____ _____ _____

  _____ _____ _____ _____ _____

Skill: Letter/Sound Connection, Labeling

Scavenger Hunt

If your child has difficulty thinking of something that starts with that Sound,

give them clues:

- I think you'll find Something that starts with the a *T* in the garage,or
- I know something that starts with a *T* that is sticky

Give extra clues to guide them to the answer.

If they are good at rhyming, give them a rhyming word.

If they are working on prepositions, Say:

- It's between the _____ and the _____.

  or

- It's next to the refrigerator.

Once they find the items, talk about them.

Ask questions:

- Where did you find it?
- What group does it belong to?
- What color is it?
- What goes with it?

Scavenger Hunt

Find things in your house that start with each letter
Some Suggestions:

B   broom, bird, bathroom, banana, bat, brush, ball, bubbles, bathtub, bag

S   Soap, scissors, Sandwich, Salad, Stairs, Soda, Salt, straw, Spoon, Sock

T   tools, toilet, toilet paper, towel, table, tissues, tennis ball, teddy bear, timer, toes

M   makeup, mirror, mom, money, medicine, music, microwave, mittens, mop, marker

What is it? I Spy Game

1.   I Spy Something in the kitchen:

      it's yellow
      you peel it
      monkeys eat it   _____

2.   I Spy Something in the garage:

      it has a handle
      you hit nails with it   _____

3.   I Spy Something in the closet:

      you wear it on your feet
      you don't wear socks
      you wear these in the summer   _____

4.   I Spy Something in the family room:

      it has buttons
      it changes the channel on tv   _____

5.   I Spy Something you play with outside:

      you kick it
      it's black and white   _____

Skill: Describing, Functions

Complete the Sentence

1. I like to eat peanut butter and _____

2. I cut my food with a _____

3. Mary had a little _____

4. I open the door with a _____

5. After I shower, I dry off with a _____

6. When you are in the car, buckle your _____

7. Give me a high _____

8. Jack and Jill went up the _____

9. Twinkle, twinkle, little _____

10. Bah, bah black _____

Skill: Sentence completion

BACK TO SCHOOL

```
S A V R M J Y L R C U Z B Z I U N
P T R A Z D G W I G M R L M E B C
R F P G X A C N S C T A U A X S R
I K B Y U Z G R I E N S R E W L A
N I G P E X O V S D I E D K J I Y
G Q O A O S K P S C A E P K E B O
B Y A H S D E U P R Z E G O U R N
R P P I J L B Z R E I O R R R A S
E K C A L L Y S I C U W Y E D R R
A S B I O G L I N E Q T J H X Y Z
K X N O O E S G C S T C H C O H I
E G H G D M G J I S R C W A U T M
G C Y E R W W N P B M O N E W A I
S N S V J T I R A V E Y Z T B M Z
X K R B N B W Z L L Q Z G X G M E
Q G T M Q W M O O R H C N U L L P
W C A R R I D E R O R C Y S X W U
```

Art Car rider Crayons Desk Gym library Lunchroom
Markers Math Music Pencil Principal Quiz Reading
Recess School bus Scissors Spring Break Teacher

Skill: Letter Identification / Visual Recognition, Reading, Vocabulary Building

67

AT THE PLAYGROUND

```
N E R D L I H C S U F R Q O A B Y
H N M A K B K P A U J E G N G Z Y
G Y G O C A L S N G K T N K R J K
Z Z K O N A R B D J B H K D U V V
I L V X Y K T B B C B G O G N R S
M O L I A H E P O S N U Y N N H J
A U N A M U I Y X G X A W E I O C
G G R M W Y S D B W I L Z W N P W
I I D W S G G L E A A D D S G S Q
N K O U F U N E I A R J W W V C E
A J M G R A N I L D N S K I J O Z
T U T Z I O R S B G E D O N R T W
I M L I E B F L H M N N S G F C A
O P K J N G C Z H I I U V E O H S
N I R F D F A J F P N L J I E E E
D N H Z S M T T E E U E C M Q K E
H G T H O U T S I D E V J Z R M S
```

**Children Climbing wall Friends Fun Hide and seek
Hopscotch Imagination Jumping Jungle gym
Laughter Monkey bars Outside Playing Running
Sandbox Seesaw Slide Sunshine Swing Tag**

Skill: Letter Identification / Visual Recognition, Reading, Vocabulary Building

PLACES TO GO

```
L D N U O R G Y A E L P E O S A G
T X P X Q Y I R A L W R C W J M R
U N J O R C E A S B A W I Q G U A
T X A E H N O C E M E M F J P S N
N Q K R A S H N U K M E F Q L E D
B A D W U O M I C I E I O Y A M P
B I A K O A D A N E Q J T N Y E A
C B I L B A T G E N R Y S P G N R
M M R E T Q P S K R R T O U R T E
M U P S U O U T E A C X P W O P N
G E O O O C K O R R V E L J U A T
O S R L R Q L B Y J T C C U N R S
T U T I A E I Z K A M C J I D K H
H M C T C L V P O H S T U N O D O
R O L R A P A Z Z I P V N S O Q U
E C I F F O S R O T C O D B O Z S
V L K O P E R A Z F N V Z K Z Y E
```

Airport Amusement Park Arena Bakery Circus
Concert Doctor's Office Donut Shop Grandparents House
Ice Cream Shop Library Museum Opera Pizza Parlor Playground
Post Office Restaurant School Stadium Swimming Pool Zoo

Skill: Letter Identification / Visual Recognition, Reading, Vocabulary Building

69

SPORTS

```
V E L L A B T O O F N D G A H T R
N W O D H C U O T U T U Q S C L Q
K F N D I I D K R D T E I O K L U
F K J V G B N E X V K N U I R A X
I Q U V G W M O C M N R N Q H B D
Z R I G H O P D R E T R Z L C T N
E E J R H R V V T H G E B F Q E C
Q C H A M P I O N P U T M U N K R
H C U Q P I Y Z G Y U N O J N S R
F O M V L G W E B V T I I N L A C
J S P F Q F B U R A R O B F C B D
V F I L U A K O E V S P L Q O B C
N L R C T W H I S T L E U D M R K
U O E O V P O O H V Q E B X H O M
J G E A P D L E I F T R C A I I V
B G D C E E R E F E R H H B L M R
L F J H F Z Z I H H P T B J U L H
```

Baseball Basketball Bat Champion Coach Court
Field Football Golf Home run Hoop Racquet
Referee Soccer Tennis Three pointer
Touchdown Umpire Uniform Whistle

Skill: Letter Identification / Visual Recognition, Reading, Vocabulary Building

70

COOKING

```
K I D O C O F F E E M A K E R Q R
R P D V G C Q V M I C R O W A V E
C P D E F J H C N L K I O H D U U
D J N N Q O I Y C D P E O O E T I
I H R S T R E F R I G E R A T O R
S Q O E L B A T I A Q S M Y E D S
H B F K W M S I L V E R W A R E E
W S R V N O R W A Y M Z A U G J I
A G Y E Q I Z J C B A L G C E F R
S A R K A S S Z K U G R S R N S E
H T T M I K T V L L P U N C T S C
E H N S H T F R T G L B O T E M O
R E A W A I C A A W G L O H T T R
K R P W Y D K H S W D M S A R B G
O I K H H E U M E T M I G N R P U
E N V N J U J Y Z N D G G E M D A
R G Y R A C E N R E T S A O T C D
```

Breakfast Coffeemaker Cold Cupboard Detergent
Dishes Dishwasher Gathering Groceries Hot
Kitchen Microwave Oven Pantry Refrigerator
Silverware Sink Straw Table Toaster

Skill: Letter Identification / Visual Recognition, Reading, Vocabulary Building

STATES

```
V K H P U A T O K A D H T R O N D
A L A B A M A X V C C K G V C T R
N X B O N U G K H O M E K A E F R
E A Y R P A R J N F O J L X P L C
W U N C D O G N J R P I A Y I O O
J N C I Y X E I G S F S U S V R L
E T O W L C Z I H O J E L E K I O
R M E T T O A T R C V B R T M D R
S N M I G X R N E J I M Y J O A A
E L C M A N I A I L O M R Q B E D
Y U A I T A I W C N A L A S K A O
T B X K I M S H T H E O N K P R V
P O O S H A A Y S V T D I C F I D
F O Q U L W W I B A H U C H V Z O
O H J L C D G A N U W S O N O O D
P T D K F C U S H E B T B S C N X
A S Y V U A C F M O N T A N A A U
```

Alabama Alaska Arizona California Colorado

Connecticut Florida Georgia Hawaii Maine

Michigan Montana New Jersey New York North Dakota

Ohio South Carolina Texas Vermont Washington

Skill: Letter Identification / Visual Recognition, Reading, Vocabulary Building

72

Preposition

Write the word under the picture that
reflects the targeted position

Over

_____

Under

_____

In front

_____

Behind

_____

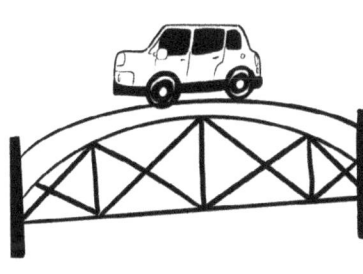

Through

_____

Skill: Grammar: Prepositions

Preposition Extension
(AKA: Positions)

Receptive Language:

Have your child move around a chair:

- Behind
- Under
- Over
- Around
- Or use 2 chairs to go between

Expressive Language:

Put yourself in a position to ask:

- Where am I? You are _____.

Skill extension:

Increased level: Add Actions:

- Slide <u>under</u> the chair
- Jump <u>over</u> the rope
- Skip <u>around</u> the table

Attributes

Dog (Example)

Category _Animal, Pet_

Location _Home, Breeder, Pet Store_

Parts _Tail, 4 Legs, Nose, Eyes_

Accessories _Leash, Collar_

Color _Any Color (Brown, Black, White, etc.)_

Size _Big, Small_

Composition _Fur_

Fire Truck

Category _____

Location _____

Parts _____

Accessories _____

Color _____

Size _____

Composition _____

Apple

Category _____

Location _____

Parts _____

Accessories _____

Color _____

Size _____

Composition _____

School

Category _____

Location _____

Parts _____

Accessories _____

Color _____

Size _____

Composition _____

Chair

Category _____

Location _____

Parts _____

Accessories _____

Color _____

Size _____

Composition _____

Skill: Expressive Vocabulary, Describing, Attributes.

What's the function?

(What do you do with____?)

1. Clock _____

2. Shoe _____

3. Keyboard _____

4. Phone _____

5. Crayons _____

6. Car _____

7. Lollipop _____

8. Hat _____

9. Ear _____

10. Piano _____

11. Flashlight _____

12. Flashlight _____

Skill: Actions

What is the action?

1. Teacher _____

2. Car _____

3. Scissors _____

4. Lawn Mower _____

5. Fan _____

6. Pencil _____

7. Phone _____

8. Vacuum _____

9. Marker _____

10. Ruler _____

Skill: Actions

Pronouns

Change the <u>underlined noun</u> to a pronoun.

1. <u>The man</u> chased the burglar away. _____

2. <u>The woman</u> bought new sunglasses. _____

3. <u>The children</u> Swam in the pool. _____

4. <u>The puppy</u> is very excited. _____

5. <u>The teacher</u> taught me Something new today. _____

6. <u>My family</u> went to the zoo to See the animals. _____

7. My mom gave <u>me and my friends</u> a Snack after school. _____

8. <u>My sister and I</u> gave the workers Some water. _____

9. It was a fun day celebrating my <u>girlfriend's</u> birthday. _____

10. I saw <u>my brother</u> Score a touchdown yesterday. _____

Skill: Grammar: Pronouns

Changing Verbs to Nouns
Someone who (Verb) is a (Noun)

1. Someone who <u>paints</u> is a _____

2. Someone who <u>drives a bus</u> is a _____

3. Someone who <u>writes</u> is a _____

4. Someone who <u>teaches</u> is a _____

5. Someone who <u>dives</u> is a _____

6. Someone who <u>jumps</u> is a _____

7. Someone who <u>sings</u> is a _____

8. Someone who <u>talks</u> is a _____

9. Someone who <u>builds</u> is a _____

10. Someone who <u>Swims</u> is a _____

11. Someone who <u>reads</u> is a _____

Skill: Converting verbs to nouns

What word describes the noun?

1. Banana _____

2. Motorcycle _____

3. Airplane _____

4. Dog _____

5. Water _____

6. Peach _____

7. Cookie _____

8. Bus _____

9. Teacher _____

10. Car _____

Skill: Adjectives

Yes or No Questions
(circle the answer)

1. Do you read a book?   Yes   No

2. Do you cook a mug?   Yes   No

3. Do you put a shoe in the oven?   Yes   No

4. Do you use a sock to stay dry in the rain?   Yes   No

5. Do you use a saw to cut food?   Yes   No

6. Is a knife sharp?   Yes   No

7. Is a pillow hard?   Yes   No

8. Can you eat a banana without peeling it?   Yes   No

9. Does a clock tell time?   Yes   No

10. Do you use a spoon to eat ice cream?   Yes   No

Skill: Answering yes/no questions

Sequencing

Write the order of the mini Story below the picture.
Think about what comes first, second, third / last.

Your school day:

_____ _____ _____

Making a meal:

_____ _____ _____

Hitting a home run:

 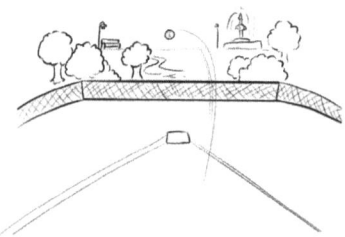 

_____ _____ _____

Skill: Sequencing and Ordinal Numbers.

Sequencing Extension

Think of activities you do during the day or weekend.
Create a list in the order you complete them.

Your school day:

_____
_____
_____
_____

Your weekend:

_____
_____
_____
_____

Making your lunchbox for school:

_____
_____
_____
_____

Making dinner:

_____
_____
_____
_____

Choosing a movie to watch:

_____
_____
_____
_____

List the steps

List the steps to complete the activities listed

1. Make a peanut butter and jelly sandwich

    _____
    _____
    _____
    _____

2. Make an ice cream sundae

    _____
    _____
    _____
    _____

3. Tie your shoes

    _____
    _____
    _____
    _____

4. Make a phone call

    _____
    _____
    _____
    _____

5. Ride a bike

    _____
    _____
    _____
    _____

Skill: Receptive Language, Sequencing with ordinal concepts. (First, Next, Last, etc.)

Same and Different

Find the word that is incorrect and write the correct
word on the line that makes the Sentence true.

1. Apple   S:_____

    Orange   D:_____

                   _____

2. Eyeglasses   S:_____

    Sunglasses   D:_____

                   _____

3. Dog   S:_____

    Cat   D:_____

                   _____

4. Frog   S:_____

    Kangaroo   D:_____

                   _____

5. Crayon   S:_____

    Marker   D:_____

                   _____

Skill: Similarities & Differences

6. Book

   Newspaper

S:_____

D:_____

_____

7. Book

   Newspaper

S:_____

D:_____

_____

8. Knife

   Saw

S:_____

D:_____

_____

9. Red

   Blue

S:_____

D:_____

_____

10. Fork

    Spoon

S:_____

D:_____

_____

11. Airplane

    Sailboat

S:_____

D:_____

_____

Semantic Absurdities

Find the word that is incorrect and write the correct
word on the line that makes the Sentence true.

1. Lock the door with a shoe. _____

2. Fly a banana on a windy day. _____

3. Drive the car with a clock. _____

4. Wash your dishes in the washing machine. _____

5. Answer the pineapple when it rings. _____

6. Wash your clothes in the dishwasher. _____

7. Wear Socks to protect your eyes. _____

8. Drink the juice with a shoelace. _____

9. Wear a hat on your foot. _____

10. Turn on the refrigerator to bake the cookies. _____

_____

Reasoning

1. Why do we put a stamp on a letter? _____

2. Why do we put ice cream in the freezer? _____

3. Why do we put the cap on the marker? _____

4. Why do we brush our hair? _____

5. Why do we mow the grass? _____

6. Why do we brush our teeth? _____

7. Why do we take medicine? _____

8. Why do we say thank you? _____

9. Why do you take an airplane instead of a car to travel? _____

_____

10. Why do people have jobs? _____

_____

Skill: WHY Questions, Reasoning and Logic

What goes together and why?

1. Teacher   School   House   Car

   Why? _____

2. Cereal   Plate   Fork   Bowl

   Why? _____

3. Pool   Bathing Suit   Shampoo   Shower

   Why? _____

4. Carpet   Door   Vacuum   Broom

   Why? _____

5. Garage   Fence   Driveway   Yard

   Why? _____

6. Bathroom   Mirror   Reflection   Picture

   Why? _____

Skill: Receptive and Expressive Vocabulary

What goes together and why?

7. Rain   Shoes   Umbrella   Dry

    Why? _____

8. Flashlight   Plug   Batteries   Charger

    Why? _____

9. Library   Gym   Books   Video

    Why? _____

10. Bus   Teacher   Road   Playground

    Why? _____

11. Straw   Medicine   cup   knife

    Why? _____

12. Spoon   Carrots   ice cream   plate

    Why? _____

Skill: Receptive and Expressive Vocabulary

Written Expression

Look at the images from the coloring pages or embedded pictures and write a sentence for each.

A _____

_____

B _____

_____

C _____

_____

D _____

_____

E _____

_____

F _____

_____

G _____

_____

H _____

_____

I _____

_____

J _____

_____

Skill: Written Expression / Sentence Formulation

Written Expression

K _____

_____

L _____

_____

M _____

_____

N _____

_____

O _____

_____

P _____

_____

Q _____

_____

R _____

_____

S _____

_____

T _____

_____

Skill: Written Expression / Sentence Formulation

Written Expression

U _____
_____

V _____
_____

W _____
_____

X _____
_____

Y _____
_____

Z _____
_____

Embedded Pictures - page 52-53

_____

_____

_____

_____

_____

_____

Skill: Written Expression / Sentence Formulation

Creating Sentences

Write a Sentence using all 3 words.

1.   Dry   Raincoat   Storm

_____

_____

2.   Sunglasses   Beach   Sister

_____

_____

3.   Book   Librarian   Friend

_____

_____

4.   Alarm   School   Late

_____

_____

5.   Teacher   Piano   Recital

_____

_____

Skill: Sentence formulation

Writing A Letter

Write a 'thank you' letter to someone.
Be sure to use capitals and punctuation where needed.

Dear_____

_____

_____

_____

_____

_____

_____

_____

_____

_____

_____

_____

_____

_____

_____

_____

Sincerely,

_____

Skill: Letter Writing and Written Expression

Practicing Greetings

What can you say when you answer the phone?

_____

What can you say when you answer the door?

_____

What can you say when you see your teacher in the morning?

_____

If someone says, "How are you?" What do you say?

_____

What can you say in return?

_____

What could you ask someone if you can tell they look sad?

_____

What compliment can you give a friend to make them feel better?

_____

What do you say to your friends at the end of the day?

_____

Enlist the help of your neighbors, family and friends to encourage vocalization, turn taking, and conversation when they meet your child.

Skill: Social interactions, Asking/Answering questions, Turn taking, Conversation

Concept of Time - Before and After

What do you do:

1. After you wake up _____

2. Before you leave for School _____

3. Before you go to bed_____

4. After you get out of the bath/shower_____

5. Before you go to the pool_____

6. Before you mail a letter_____

7. After you get home from school _____

8. Before you brush your teeth_____

9. After you are done with dinner_____

10. After you wash your clothes_____

Skill: Before and After

97

Calendar

Directions:

At the start of each month, put the numbers on the calendar

* Discuss what activities you have planned.

* Talk about the days of the week.

* What is happening at the beginning, middle and end of the month or what happens first, second, last, before/after another event?

* If you're going on a trip, talk about how many days it will last, where you have to go, and who you will See.

Sunday	Monday	Tuesday	Wednesday	Thursday	Friday	Saturday

Skill: Sequencing, Before and After, Numbers, Concept of Time.

Inferences

For each situation, identify what the situation is telling you.

You ring the doorbell and no one answers.

_____

The washing machine Signal went off.

_____

The table at the restaurant isn't ready yet.

_____

You call Someone on the phone, and there is no answer.

_____

The plant is dry, and the leaves are falling off.

_____

The kid keeps falling off the bike because he can't put his feet on the ground.

_____

The Smoke detector went off.

_____

The dogs are barking and looking out the window.

_____

The printer Stopped printing the document.

_____

You show up at the bus stop late, and no one is there.

_____

Skill: Inferencing, Higher level thinking

Game Suggestions

UNO – If you are playing **UNO** and the **ACTIVE** cards are too difficult for your child, reduce the deck to just the **COLORS** and work on matching numbers and colors.

CONNECT FOUR – Play the game but have them answer a question before they take a turn.

CHUTES & LADDERS – Play the game and have them earn a turn doing something like a question card or practicing vocabulary before they take a turn. Use whatever goals they are working on and incorporate them into their turn!

GO FISH – Great game to address sounds, take turns, answer questions, formulate questions, label vocabulary.

I SPY – Play while in the car, taking a trip or going somewhere. Create a ritual in the car by asking about their day, what they did, who they saw, etc. and make it fun!!! Turn it into a game and have them describe what they did without saying it specifically and see if you can guess!!

MADLIBS – Great way to get kids naming parts of speech and thinking of items in the categories needed, then reading the story and seeing how funny it sounds!

A BIT OF BANTER JR. – a great game for conversation skills

TABOO – to develop vocabulary, schematic thinking, and expressive language

OUTBURST JUNIOR - to develop vocabulary, schematic thinking, and expressive language

IMAGINIFF JR. - great for developing episodic memory and abstract, inferential thinking skills

AMERICAN GIRL 300 WISHES – great for social skills, forming opinions, and making decisions

BREAK THE SAFE - amazing collaborative social skills game: you will need to find on eBay

OODLES OF DOODLES - to develop vocabulary, schematic thinking, and visual imagery skills

STARE JUNIOR – for episodic memory, attention, and schematic thinking

WHOONU - great for social skills, forming opinions, and making decisions

SYNC UP - great for social skills, schematic thinking, and expressive language

REMOTE CONTROL IMPULSE CONTROL, FRANKLIN LEARNING SYSTEMS - a great game for teaching impulse control and self-regulation

APPLES TO APPLES- develops verbal organization and semantic feature analysis skills

PICTIONARY AND PICTIONARY MAN - develop visual-motor construction and formulation of "future picture" thinking

SCATTEGORIES - develop verbal organization and word retrieval skills at the word level

TRIBOND JUNIOR - develop flexible thinking and verbal organization skills at the word level

RAT A TAT CAT - reinforce visual-spatial skills and working memory

CHARADES FOR KIDS - to facilitate nonverbal expression and gestural communication

BLOKUS - to develop visual-spatial, visual working memory, and problem-solving skills

BOTTOM LINE – You do not need to follow the rules of a game to a tee. You can tweak them to work for you in whatever capacity your child is able to engage. As they grow and learn, you can start to use the game more specifically how it was intended if you desire.

Skill: Turn taking, Listening, Receptive language, Following directions, Matching, Color and Number recognition, Vocabulary, Expressive language, Articulation

Suggested answers for:

- **Rhyming page**
    - **Cat** – bat, rat, hat
    - **Star** – bar, car, far
    - **Spoon** – moon, noon, dune
    - **Bug** – rug, hug, tug
    - **Lash** – rash, bash, trash
    - **Ice** – mice, nice, vice
    - **Type** – hype, ripe, pipe
    - **Foam** – home, dome, roam
    - **Ran** – fan, man, can
    - **Fair** – bear, care, stare

- **What's the function**
    - **Clock** – tell time
    - **Shoe** – protect feet
    - **Keyboard** – type
    - **Phone** – call, talk
    - **Crayons** – color, draw
    - **Car** – drive
    - **Lollipop** – lick
    - **Hat** – wear it
    - **Ear** – hear, listen
    - **Piano** – make music, play
    - **Flashlight** – see in the dark
    - **Knife** – cut food

- **Words that describe the noun**
    - Soft, yellow, curved – **Banana**
    - Fast, dangerous, loud – **Motorcycle**
    - Heavy, large, fast – **Airplane**
    - Furry, playful – **Dog**
    - Wet, refreshing, cold – **Water**
    - Tasty, juicy, soft, pink – **Peach**
    - Crunchy, round – **Cookie**
    - Big, yellow, long, school – **Bus**
    - Smart, pretty – **Teacher**
    - Any color, big, small – **Car**

- **Changing verb to noun**
    - **Paints** – painter
    - **Drives a bus** – bus driver
    - **Writes** – writer
    - **Teaches** – teacher
    - **Dives** – diver
    - **Jumps** – jumper
    - **Sings** – singer
    - **Builds** – builder
    - **Swims** – swimmer
    - **Reads** – reader

- **Change Nouns to Pronouns**
    - **The man** – He
    - **The woman** – She
    - **The children** – They

- o **The teacher – He/She**
- o **My family – We**
- o **My friends – us**
- o **My girlfriend – her**
- o **My brother – him**

- **Inferences**
  - o **Doorbell - no one is home.**
  - o **Washing Machine - the load is ready/done**
  - o **Table isn't ready - the people at the table aren't done eating to make our table available.**
  - o **No answer - not able to answer the phone/they are busy.**
  - o **Plant is dry- the plant needs water. It is unhealthy.**
  - o **Kid falling off bike - the seat is too high/needs to lower it.**
  - o **Smoke detector - something is burning in the house (food in the oven is burning, or there's a fire!)**
  - o **Dogs are barking - someone is outside the window and catches the dog's attention.**
  - o **Printer stopped - the printer is out of paper or there is a paper jam.**
  - o **No one at the bus stop - you missed the bus.**

App Suggestions

1. <u>Monkey PK</u> – works on basic concepts, following directions, listening.

2. <u>Articulation Station Hive</u> – while a great articulation app that works on all sounds, it is also beneficial to labeling pictures and understanding stories, engaging in conversation by all the added layers to this app!

3. <u>Osmo</u> – works on letter recognition, number recognition, tangrams, following directions, stories (based on the games you buy)

4. <u>Bag Game</u> – helps you work on categories, ask questions, answer yes/no.

5. <u>Hearbuilder</u> (my clients gain access through my subscription) as it has 4 different apps - sequencing, following direction, auditory memory and phonological awareness.

6. <u>Kangaroo Island</u> – works on categories and understanding how items go together.

7. <u>Wet, Dry, Try</u> is an app made by "Handwriting Without Tears" company that helps kids learn to write letters properly.

8. <u>Endless ABC</u> helps kids put letters together to spell words while the sound is made.

9. <u>Fun & Functional</u> – Helps kids answer questions receptively but then speak the answer expressively immediately after (you can adjust settings as needed)

10. <u>Auditory Workout</u> – requires kids to listen and follow directions. Each level gets more advanced with concepts of "before/after," using prepositions and colors etc.

11. <u>Preposition Builder</u> – This app has kids label/fill in the blank with the right position while reading the sentence and looking at a picture prompt.

Documentation Pages

Date	Skill Practiced	Outcome/Result

Documentation Pages

Date	Skill Practiced	Outcome/Result

Documentation Pages

Date	Skill Practiced	Outcome/Result

INDEX

A quick guide to finding the skills you want to work on.

- **Time Concept**
  - Calendar - page 98
  - Before/After - pages 96,97

- **Turn-Taking**
  - Conversations - page 96
  - Greetings - page 96
  - Hopscotch - page 58

- **Vocabulary Building**
  1. Lists - page 61
  2. Things that Go Together - page 54,89
  3. Rhyming - page 55
  4. Opposites - pages 56,57
  5. Categories - pages 59,61
  6. Making lists - page 61
  7. Scavenger Hunt - pages 62,63,64
  8. I SPY - page 65
  9. Completing the Sentence - page 66
  10. Word Searches - pages 67,68,69,70,72,72
  11. Attributes - Page 75
  12. Functions - pages 65,76
  13. Changing Verbs to Nouns - page 79
  14. Labeling items on shape pages - pages 42,43,44,45
  15. Labeling pictures on the letter/sound connection pages - pages 46,47,48
  16. Same/Different - pages 85,86

Final Thoughts

As you moved through this book, I hope you learned new ways to approach talking and interacting with your child.

Any activity can be both receptive and expressive - it's all in how you present the information. Receptive learning is listening and interpreting what you are saying, but engaging your child verbally turns it into an expressive activity. Therefore, your child may know and understand what you are saying but not be able to use the words on their own yet - and that's ok! Creating receptive understanding is KEY to building expressive language!!

I hope this book is the catalyst for you and your child to find endless opportunities in making learning fun!!

Remember to be consistent as practice makes progress!
Happy learning!

Robyn